# WILD WORK

# WHO WALKS IN SPACE?

## WORKING IN SPACE

Linda Tagliaferro

**www.raintreepublishers.co.uk**
Visit our website to find out
more information about
Raintree books.

**To order:**
☎ Phone 0845 6044371
🖷 Fax +44 (0) 1865 312263
🖳 Email myorders@raintreepublishers.co.uk

Customers from outside the UK please telephone +44 1865 312262

Raintree is an imprint of Capstone Global Library Limited,
a company incorporated in England and Wales having its
registered office at 7 Pilgrim Street, London, EC4V 6LB –
Registered company number: 6695582

Edited by David Andrews, Nancy Dickmann, and Rebecca
Rissman
Designed by Victoria Allen
Picture research by Liz Alexander
Leveled by Marla Conn, with Read-Ability.
Originated by Dot Gradations Ltd
Printed and bound in China by Leo Paper Products

ISBN  978 1 4062 1678 3 (hardback)
14 13 12 11 10
10 9 8 7 6 5 4 3 2 1

**British Library Cataloguing in Publication Data**
Tagliaferro, Linda.
  Who walks in space? : working in space. -- (Wild
work)
  1. Astronauts--Juvenile literature. 2. Space shuttles--
Juvenile literature. 3. Space stations--Juvenile
literature.
  I. Title II. Series
  629.4'5'023-dc22

**Acknowledgements**
The author and publisher are grateful to the following for
permission to reproduce copyright material:
Alamy pp. 5 (© Stocktrek Images, Inc.), 26 (© NASA); Corbis
pp. 6 (© Roger Ressmeyer), 7 (© Scott Andrews/Science
Faction), 10 (© NASA/Roger Ressmeyer), 11 (© NASA/
Reuters), 13 (© Sergei Chirikov/epa), 17, 19, 20 (© Bettmann),
29 (© Bettmann); Getty Images pp. 8 (Mark Wilson), 12 (Bill
Ingalls/AFP), 18 (John Nordell/Christian Science Monitor),
28 (Bruce Weaver/AFP); NASA pp. 4, 21, 27; Photolibrary
pp. 23 (NASA/age footstock), 25 (White); Reuters p. 15
(NASA); Science Photo Library pp. 9 (NASA), 14 (Detlev Van
Ravenswaay), 16 (NASA), 22 (NASA), 24 (NASA).

Background design features reproduced with permission of
© CORBIS. Cover photograph reproduced with permission
of Shutterstock (© trucic).

Every effort has been made to contact copyright holders
of material reproduced in this book. Any omissions will
be rectified in subsequent printings if notice is given to
the publisher.

All the Internet addresses (URLs) given in this book were valid
at the time of going to press. However, due to the dynamic
nature of the Internet, some addresses may have changed, or
sites may have changed or ceased to exist since publication.
While the author and publisher regret any inconvenience this
may cause readers, no responsibility for any such changes can
be accepted by either the author or the publisher.

Some words are shown in bold, **like this**. You can find
out what they mean by looking in the glossary.

**DID YOU KNOW?**
A space shuttle can be taller than an 18-storey building!

Many people work together to **launch** a space shuttle. Then **astronauts** can live and work safely in space.

# Launching a space shuttle

People who work in **ground control** help **astronauts** take off and land. They make sure everything is safe before they **launch**, or take off. They check if bad weather is on the way.

## DID YOU KNOW?

Thousands of people work together in ground control.

If there are problems, ground
control stops the launch. They
make sure all problems are fixed
so that the astronauts are safe.

# The commander

Before a **space shuttle** is **launched**, the commander makes sure the crew is well trained.

commander

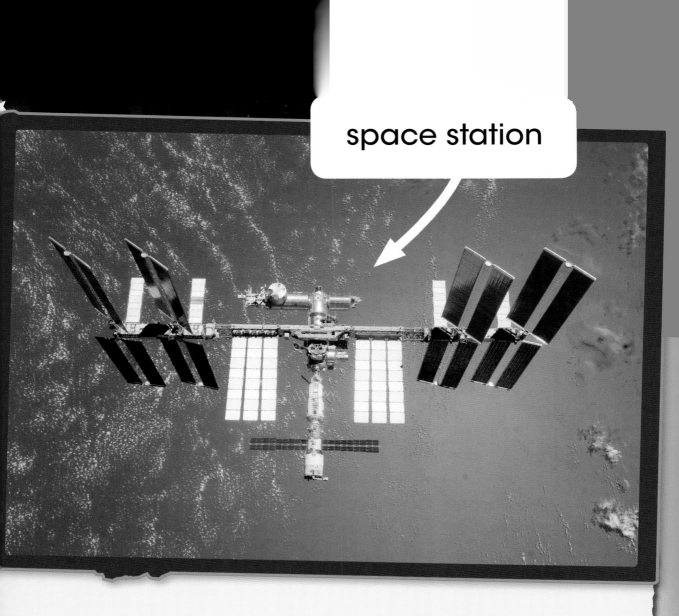

space station

The pilot **docks** the shuttle. This means the shuttle attaches to the space station. Then astronauts can safely walk into the space station.

# Keeping in touch

**Astronauts** can live in the **International Space Station** for months. The station flies 400 kilometres (250 miles) high in an **orbit** around Earth. But they are always communicating with **ground control**. They can talk to people on the ground through a video connection.

# o makes dinner in space?

dinner, **astronauts** go to the
ley, or kitchen. They add hot
er to dry food in pouches.
ne food is fresh, such as fruit.

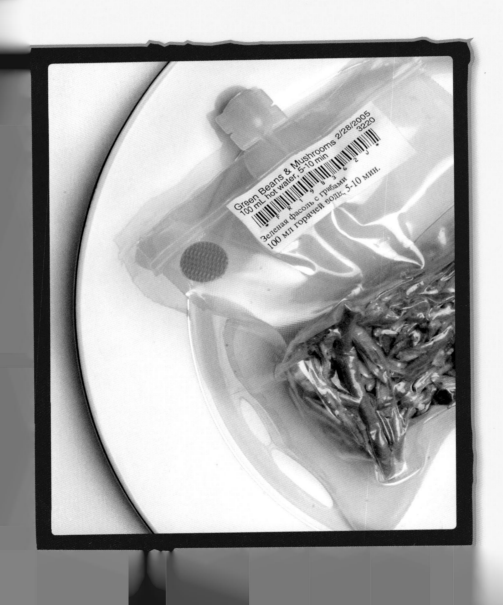

## DID YOU KNOW?

Astronauts strap themselves to a treadmill to exercise. They also use machines with pedals like bicycles to use their leg muscles.

## Joysticks in space

**Canadarm2** is a robot "arm" on the outside of the space station. An **astronaut** looks at screens and uses a joystick to move the arm. Canadarm2 can move big pieces of equipment from one place to another.

joystick

Canadarm2

# Walking in space

Sometimes **astronauts** walk outside the **space station**. Space has no air. It is dark and cold. One astronaut helps another into a protective suit.

## DID YOU KNOW?

Just in case astronauts need to go to the toilet on a space walk, they wear a special nappy!

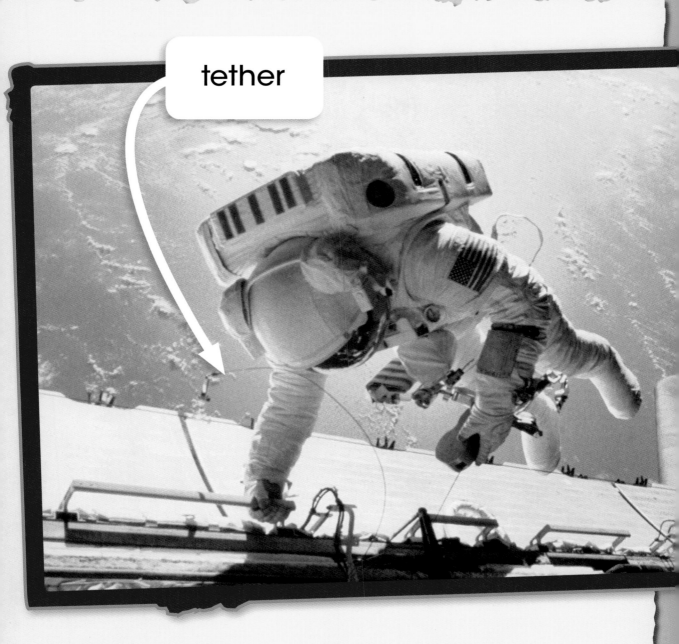

tether

Astronauts are attached to the
space station by a strong rope
called a **tether**.

# Landing a space shuttle

A **space shuttle** circles, or **orbits**, Earth. It travels at about 28,200 kilometres (17,500 miles) per hour. That's 35 times faster than an aeroplane! To return to Earth, the commander must use controls to slow it down. The commander then lands the space shuttle like a plane.

## DID YOU KNOW?

A big parachute opens behind the space shuttle when it lands. This helps to slow it down.

# Could you work in space?

Would you like to explore space? To work in a space station, you must be able to make quick decisions. You need to study **astronomy**, maths, and other subjects.

# Find out more

## Books to read

*Living in Space*, Patricia Whitehouse (Heinemann Library, 2005)

See Inside Space, Katie Daynes (Usborne, 2008)

*Working in Space*, Patricia Whitehouse (Heinemann Library, 2005)

## Websites to visit

**www.kidsastronomy.com/space_shuttle.htm**
Learn about spaces shuttles and all their different parts.

**http://iss.jaxa.jp/kids/en/life/index.html**
Get answers to your questions about eating, sleeping, and more in space.

**http://www.spacecentre.co.uk**
Visit the National Space Centre in Leicester or go to its website to find out more about space and astronauts.

# Index

Newport Community Learning & Libraries
Cymuned ddysgu a Llyfrgelloedd Casnewydd

THIS ITEM SHOULD BE RETURNED OR
RENEWED BY THE LAST DATE
STAMPED BELOW

Newport
CITY COUNCIL
CYNGOR DINAS
Casnewydd

Bettws Library & Information Centre
Tel: 656656

J

17 FEB 2012

09 JAN 2015
27 AUG 2015

To renew telephone 656656 or 656657 (minicom)
or www.newport.gov.uk/libraries